Social Studies Explorer

DEMOCRATIC REPUBLIC OF THE CONGO

◆ by G. S. Prentzas

CHERRY LAKE PUBLISHING • ANN ARBOR, MICHIGAN

Published in the United States of America
by Cherry Lake Publishing
Ann Arbor, Michigan
www.cherrylakepublishing.com

Content Adviser: Laura Seay, PhD, Assistant Professor, Department of Political Science, Morehouse College, Atlanta, Georgia

Book design and production: The Design Lab

Photo credits: Cover, ©Antonella865/Dreamstime.com; cover (stamp), ©dicogm/Shutterstock, Inc.; page 4, ©Zute Lightfoot/Alamy; pages 5, 27, and 28, ©Robert Harding Picture Library Ltd/Alamy; page 8, ©Robert Harding World Imagery/Alamy; pages 9 and 35, ©matt griggs/Alamy; page 11, ©National Geographic Image Collection/Alamy; pages 12, 18, 21, 31, 32, 33, and 36, ©ASSOCIATED PRESS; page 14, ©imagebroker/Alamy; pages 15 and 17, ©North Wind Picture Archives/Alamy; pages 19, ©Bettmann/Corbis/AP Images; page 20, ©Allstar Picture Library/Alamy; page 23, ©Iakov Filimonov/Shutterstock, Inc.; page 24, ©blinow61/Shutterstock, Inc.; page 25, ©ZUMA Wire Service/Alamy; page 40, ©Robert Fried/Alamy; page 45, ©bonchan/Shutterstock, Inc.

Library of Congress Cataloging-in-Publication Data
Prentzas, G. S.
   It's cool to learn about countries. Democratic Republic of the Congo/by G. S. Prentzas.
      p. cm.—(Social studies explorer)
   Includes bibliographical references and index.
   ISBN 978-1-61080-443-1 (lib. bdg.) — ISBN 978-1-61080-530-8 (e-book) —
ISBN 978-1-61080-617-6 (pbk.)
1. Congo (Democratic Republic)—Juvenile literature. I. Title. II. Title: Democratic Republic
of Congo.
   DT644.P74 2012
   967.51—dc23   2012002617

Cherry Lake Publishing would like to acknowledge the work of The Partnership for
21st Century Skills. Please visit www.21stcenturyskills.org for more information.

Printed in the United States of America
Corporate Graphics Inc.
July 2012
CLFA11

TABLE OF CONTENTS

Democratic Republic of the **Congo**

CHAPTER ONE
Welcome to the Congo! 4

CHAPTER TWO
Business and Government 14

CHAPTER THREE
Meet the People 27

CHAPTER FOUR
Celebrations! 33

CHAPTER FIVE
What's for Dinner? 40

Glossary 46
For More Information......47
Index 48
About the Author 48

CHAPTER ONE

WELCOME TO THE CONGO!

➥ Kinshasa is the capital of the Democratic Republic of the Congo.

Would you like to explore the Democratic Republic of the Congo? Then get ready to travel down one of the world's longest rivers and across several different types of landscapes. The story of the Congo goes back thousands of years. Ancient peoples built powerful

kingdoms in this central African country. Today, between 65 million and 72 million people call the Democratic Republic of the Congo home.

What type of land do you imagine when you think of the Congo? If you're picturing tropical forests and grasslands that are home to African wildlife, you're right! But the country also has large lakes and snow-covered mountains.

The Democratic Republic of the Congo stretches across 905,568 square miles (2.34 million square kilometers). That makes it about one-fourth the size of the United

↞ Congolese people often travel along the Congo River using handmade boats.

States. The Congo is the second-largest country in Africa and the eleventh-largest in the world. The Republic of the Congo lies to the northwest of the Democratic Republic of the Congo. Although the name of this former French **colony** looks similar, the Republic of the Congo is a separate country. The Central African Republic and South Sudan sit along the Congo's northern and north-eastern borders. Uganda, Rwanda, and Burundi form most of the Congo's eastern border. Also to the east, Lake Tanganyika sits between the Congo and Tanzania. Zambia and Angola lie to the south. The Congo's western edge is a 25-mile (40 km) strip of coastline along the Atlantic Ocean.

Kinshasa, the nation's capital, is located on the banks of the Congo River in the western part of the country. It is about 320 miles (515 km) from the Atlantic Ocean. More than 8 million people, more than 10 percent of the entire country's population, live in Kinshasa. It is the third-largest city in Africa.

The Congo River is the main geographical feature in the Democratic Republic of the Congo. Its **basin** stretches across most of the country and makes up more than 10 percent of the entire continent of Africa! Millions of years ago, the Congo Basin was a huge lake. Hills and mountain ranges surrounded it. Today, the Congo River and its many **tributaries** are all that remain of this ancient lake. The

Congo River reaches about 2,900 miles (4,667 km) from its source in northern Zambia. It flows north and then curves west before turning southwest and pouring into the Atlantic Ocean. Some of the most remote wildernesses in the world are located along the banks of the Congo River.

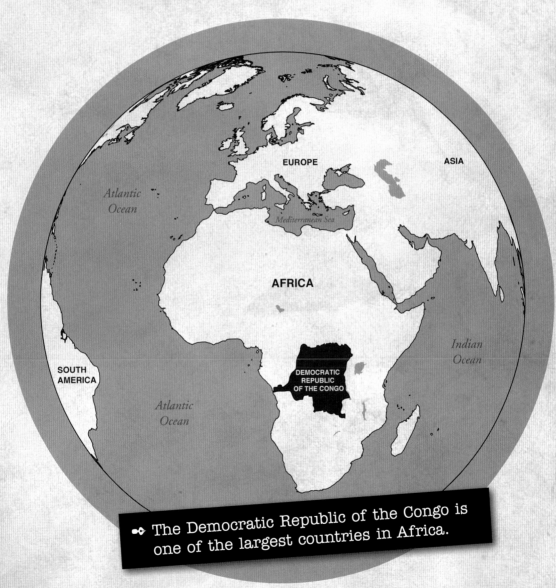

⬩ The Democratic Republic of the Congo is one of the largest countries in Africa.

➼ Mount Nyiragongo is one of the active volcanoes of the Virunga Mountains.

A large area of lowlands lies in the center of the Congo. Some of this land is wet and swampy. Dense tropical rain forests cover higher ground. Savannas lie in the south and southwest. Savannas are huge areas of grassy land. They are usually dry, so only small trees and bushes grow in them. The western and eastern regions of the Congo feature high mountains. People usually don't think of snow when they think of Africa, but the peaks of the Rwenzori Mountains are capped with snow all year. The Virunga

Mountains along the Congo's eastern border are a chain of volcanoes. Two of the volcanoes still belch smoke regularly.

The Congo has many large lakes. Lake Tanganyika is the world's longest lake. It stretches for 420 miles (676 km) along the Congo's eastern border. Other major lakes include Lake Mweru, Lake Albert, and Lake Edward.

What do you need to pack if you plan to visit the Democratic Republic of the Congo? If you're thinking summer clothes and an umbrella, you are right! About one-third of the Congo lies above the **equator**, and the

➦ Congolese fishermen fish in the waters of Lake Tanganyika and other major lakes throughout the country.

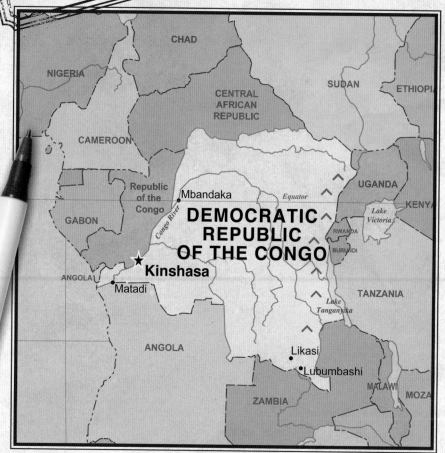

Take a close look at this map of the Democratic Republic of the Congo. Then set a separate piece of paper over it and carefully trace an outline of the country. Draw the Congo River and its major tributaries, as well as Lake Tanganyika. Mark the locations of mountain ranges. Make a line to show the location of the equator. Label the other land features that you have just read about. Draw a star to mark where Kinshasa is located. Then add in the Congo's other major cities. Think about where these cities are located. What do they have in common?

The Congo River was originally known as the Nzere, meaning "the river that swallows all rivers." Early European explorers began calling it the Congo, after the Kongo people who lived near the mouth of the river, and the new name stuck. The Congo River is the world's deepest river. At its mouth, the river's current is so strong that it has carved a huge underwater canyon in the floor of the Atlantic Ocean. This canyon stretches out almost 125 miles (201 km) from shore!

rest lies below it. Areas close to the equator have some of the warmest weather on earth, so much of the country is hot and humid year-round. Average temperatures range between 70 degrees Fahrenheit (21 degrees Celsius) and 80°F (26.6°C) in most parts of the country. The weather is much cooler in the higher plateaus and mountains. Throughout the country, the temperature varies little from month to month.

Instead of winter, spring, summer, and fall, the Congo has two seasons—rainy and dry. South of the equator, the rainy season lasts from November to March. North of the Equator, it lasts from April to October. The average annual rainfall for the entire country is about 42 inches (107 centimeters). Some areas get more than 80 inches (203 cm) per year. That's a lot of rain!

The Democratic Republic of the Congo is home to more than 10,000 plant **species**, 1,000 bird species,

❧ Okapis have striped legs that make them look somewhat like zebras.

and 400 mammal species. The country has more types of plants and animals than any other African country.

The lush tropical rain forests that surround the Congo River and its tributaries are home to many tall trees. Mahogany, palm, ebony, and limba are some of the soaring trees that form a canopy high above the floor of the rain forest. Because these trees block out so much sunlight, only certain plants are able to grow in the rich soil beneath them. Many different types of ferns and flowering vines grow in the rain forest. The African violet is another type of plant that grows well in the shade. Many different types of grasses cover the country's savannas. Farmers grow coconut palms and banana trees for their fruits. In the southern Congo, the huge Bangweulu Swamps wetland area is home to reeds and marsh plants. These plants soak up the river water like a sponge, slowing the flow of the river.

Familiar animals such as elephants, giraffes, lions, hippopotamuses, rhinoceroses, and crocodiles all live in the Congo. Unusual animals, including the okapi, also make the Congo home. The okapi is related to the giraffe, but it looks more like a cross between an antelope and a zebra. The Congo is perhaps best known for its **primates**. Chimpanzees, baboons, bonobos, gorillas, and colobus monkeys are some of the primates that live in the Congo. Many types of birds, including flamingos and spoonbills, live in the country's swampy areas.

CHAPTER TWO

BUSINESS AND GOVERNMENT

❧ The Luba people created wooden masks and other interesting artifacts.

People have lived in what is now the Congo for at least 10,000 years. Around 1000 BCE, new groups of people moved into the region from the areas north of the Congo. By the 1300s CE, the Kongo Kingdom had established itself along the mouth of the Congo River. The Luba and Lunda Kingdoms ruled in the east. These

groups fought against each other to gain control of the central part of the country.

Portuguese explorers arrived in the Congo in 1482. They traded their goods to the Kongo people in exchange for ivory and other items. The Portuguese later brought corn, tobacco, and cassava to the Kongo Kingdom. These three crops became important to the people of the Congo. In the 1500s, slaves became a major part of the trade between European countries and the Kongo. The Kongo captured prisoners in their battles with the Luba and other

◦• Many African people were captured and sold into slavery after Europeans began trading with Africans.

enemies. Then they traded the prisoners to the Europeans. European ships carried the enslaved people to the Caribbean islands and the Americas. There, they were sold to European colonists and forced to work on plantations.

In the 1870s, King Leopold of Belgium read about the explorer Henry Stanley's travels along the Congo River. Several European countries had already established colonies in Africa. Leopold wanted to have a colony as well. In 1885, he created the Congo Free State. Ignoring the native people and their rulers, Leopold declared the area as his own. Unlike other European colonies in Africa, the Congo Free State was not a colony of the Belgian government. It was the personal property of Leopold himself.

Leopold sent soldiers to enforce his rule over the Congo. He also sent merchants and missionaries. The merchants began shipping the Congo's valuable ivory, lumber, and other natural resources to Europe. Although Leopold and the missionaries built schools and hospitals, the Congo Free State era was a terrible time for the people of the Congo. Belgian soldiers forced them to build roads and railroads, which were needed to transport raw materials out of the jungle. When cars become more popular at the beginning of the 20th century, the demand for rubber tires soared. The rain forests of the Congo had many rubber plants. The Belgians forced Congolese men, women, and children to work on rubber plantations and collect rubber from the jungle.

◄► Henry Stanley's travels in the Congo inspired King Leopold of Belgium to begin colonizing the area.

When missionaries working in the Congo returned to Europe, they told stories about how badly Leopold's men treated the Congolese. The Belgian legislature voted to take the colony from Leopold. It renamed the colony the Belgian Congo and eventually ended the practice of forced labor. Belgian Congo officials eventually began allowing Congolese people to own land and to take part in the colony's government. During the 1940s and 1950s, many Congolese moved from rural areas to cities. The cities offered more jobs than rural areas.

In the late 1950s, European colonies throughout Africa began gaining independence. The first independence movement in the Belgian Congo started in 1956. In 1960, after a four-year struggle, the Republic of Congo declared its independence from Belgium. Patrice Lumumba was elected as the country's first prime minister. Joseph Kasavubu was selected as its first president. The new country faced many problems. Many different **ethnic** groups lived in the Congo. They could not agree on how to run the country. Violent, deadly conflicts soon flared up among the groups.

↝ Joseph Kasavubu (left) and Patrice Lumumba (right) led the Congo in its earliest days as an independent nation.

Joseph Mobutu (right) took over leadership of the Congo in late 1960.

Army leader Joseph Mobutu staged a **coup** in September 1960. Prime Minister Lumumba was imprisoned and later killed. Over the next five years, three different politicians served as the Congo's president. As head of the army, Mobutu held the real power. In 1965, Mobutu took full control of the government. He soon became a harsh dictator. For more than 30 years, his army threatened or killed anyone who opposed him. Mobutu also became very wealthy. Much of the money from the Congo's industries went to him instead of to the Congolese people.

In 1994, ethnic violence in neighboring Rwanda spilled over into the Congo. Between 1 million and 2 million refugees poured into the country. They brought their tribal disputes with them. Refugee **militias** fought against each other and the Congo's army. Rebel groups made up of Congolese people opposing Mobutu also joined the battle. Civilians were caught in the crossfire between these warring groups.

In 1972, Joseph Mobutu changed his name to Mobutu Sese Seko Koko Ngbendu Wa Za Banga. The previous year, he had officially renamed the Congo River the Zaire River, one of its ancient names. Mobutu also changed the name of the country from the Republic of Congo to the Republic of Zaire. When Mobutu's reign ended in 1997, the name of the river was changed back to the Congo River. The country also adopted a new name, the Democratic Republic of the Congo, to distinguish itself from its neighbor, the Republic of the Congo.

↝ Laurent Kabila was president of the Congo from 1997 to 2001.

A rebel army led by Laurent Kabila began winning battles against Mobutu's forces. Kabila's army pushed Mobutu back toward Kinshasa. Sensing that events had turned against him, Mobutu fled the country in 1997. Kabila proclaimed himself president of the Congo. In 2001, for unknown reasons, he was assassinated by one of his bodyguards. Kabila's son, Joseph, was named president 10 days later. The 29-year-old was the world's youngest national leader.

The Congo adopted a new constitution in 2005 and held an election later that year. Kabila won the presidential election. He was reelected in 2011, but his opponents disputed the election. Many votes had not been counted. Many Congolese believed the election results were not legitimate.

Each of the Congo's 10 provinces has its own government. These governments handle local issues. The national government of the Democratic Republic of the Congo has three branches. A nationwide election is held to select the president, who heads the executive branch. The president serves a five-year term and appoints **cabinet** members. The president also appoints the prime minister.

The national legislature, the second branch, is divided into two groups. The Senate has 108 seats, and the National Assembly has 500 seats. The legislatures of the provinces select senators. Voters elect members of the National Assembly. Members of both houses serve five-year terms. These legislators write and adopt the country's laws.

The judiciary, the third branch, consists of several levels of courts. The Constitutional Court hears cases involving constitutional issues. The Appeals Court reviews decisions of lower courts. Civil courts try local cases.

Unfortunately, this government system does not always work the way it is supposed to. **Corruption** is a major problem throughout the nation, and **bribes** are often the only way to get anything done.

The Democratic Republic of the Congo has many valuable natural resources. Violence and political troubles have prevented the country's people from using these resources to create wealth. Between 1997 and 2007, the fighting between Congolese military groups and foreign armies contributed to the deaths of more than 5 million people in the Congo. They died as a result of violence, famine, and disease.

The Congo is one of Africa's poorest countries. Most Congolese live on less than one U.S. dollar a day.

The flag of the Democratic Republic of the Congo is blue. A thick red stripe runs diagonally from the lower left to the upper right and is bordered by two thin yellow stripes. A yellow star sits in the upper left corner. Each part of the flag represents different ideals. The blue symbolizes hope and peace. The yellow represents the country's wealth. The red stands for the blood of the country's heroes. The star symbolizes unity and a brilliant future.

The Congolese franc is the Democratic Republic of the Congo's currency. Francs come in paper money. In June 2012, one U.S. dollar was worth more than 900 Congolese francs.

Business owners are hesitant to start companies in the Congo because of safety concerns and government corruption. Government officials often go unpaid for months or even years. They make a living by demanding bribes from businesspeople to approve licenses or authorize other business activities.

Many Congolese workers are unemployed or have only part-time or seasonal jobs. About 70 percent of workers in the Congo have agricultural jobs. Farmers and farmworkers grow and produce a wide range

of goods. Coffee, sugar, palm oil, and rubber are the nation's primary agricultural products. Cotton, tea, cocoa, cassava, bananas, peanuts, corn, and fruits are also important crops.

Mining is the Congo's biggest industry. Diamonds, gold, copper, cobalt, zinc, and tin are some of the valuable minerals mining companies dig up. Most mining companies are owned by foreign businesspeople. They transport the minerals out of the country. The Congo has few factories that make goods from these minerals. As a result, only a small amount of the wealth created by Congolese mines remains in the country.

➥ Minerals are one of the Congo's most valuable natural resources.

Congolese industries also produce textiles, plastics, and other manufactured goods. The timber industry harvests valuable trees, such as mahogany and ebony. Like mining companies, most timber companies in the Congo are foreign owned. Most trees from the Congo's forests are shipped abroad.

IMPORT EXPORT

You can understand the Democratic Republic of the Congo's economy better by looking at the goods and services it imports and exports. Imports are things that a country buys from other countries. Exports are things that a country sells to other countries. Here are some of the Congo's top imports and exports:

IMPORTS ⟶	DEMOCRATIC REPUBLIC OF THE CONGO	⟶ EXPORTS
food		diamonds
mining machinery		copper
other machinery		gold
transport equipment		wood products
fuels		coffee

CHAPTER THREE

MEET THE PEOPLE

The people of the Congo live everywhere from cities such as Kisangani (above) to tiny rural villages.

Between 65 million and 72 million people live in the Democratic Republic of the Congo. More than one-third of all Congolese live in Kinshasa, Lubumbashi, Kisangani, and other cities. In rural areas, many people live along the Congo River and its tributaries or near the country's lakes. Many people also live in the country's mountainous regions.

Religion is an important part of life in the Congo. About 80 percent of the country's population is Christian. About 50 percent are Catholics and about 20 percent are Protestants. Another 10 percent are members of a Christian religion known as Kimbanguism.

About 10 percent of the Congo's population is Muslim. Muslims observe the teachings of the Prophet Muhammad. Some Congolese follow traditional religions that are thousands of years old. These ancient religions have a wide range of beliefs and rituals. Many Congolese

➥ A small portion of the Congo's population is Muslim.

who are Christian or Muslim also include traditional religious beliefs and practices in their spiritual life.

Some Congolese people visit advisers and spiritual healers known as *ngangas*. Ngangas use different herbs to cure headaches and other medical conditions. They also perform rituals to help people cope with problems. Each ritual is thought to have a specific effect. One ritual helps increase crop harvests. Another helps make a pregnancy easier for an expectant mother. Ngangas use a gourd or a special container called a *nkisi* for their rituals. The nkisi is a figure that contains herbs or other sacred items. The contents of the nkisi are thought to contain the power of deceased ancestors. Ngangas are believed to control events by using this power.

The Congo has more than 200 different ethnic groups. The largest ethnic groups are the Mongo, Luba, Kongo, and the Mangbetu-Azande. These four groups make up about 45 percent of the country's population.

The people of the Congo speak a wide variety of languages. French is the official national language. The Belgians introduced French to the Congo. It is one of Belgium's official languages. Today, French is used for official government business and in commerce. Several other languages are also recognized as national languages. In the eastern Congo, most people speak Kiswahili. Other popular languages include Lingala, Kikongo, and Tshiluba.

The French language is taught in schools and is used in many Congolese newspapers and magazines. In addition to French, many Congolese people speak and read at least one other language. It is usually an ethnic or regional language. For example, Lingala is spoken in Kinshasa and throughout northwestern Congo. Lingala started as a way for Congolese traders who spoke different languages to communicate. About 10 million people in the Democratic Republic of the Congo, the Republic of the Congo, and other nearby countries speak Lingala.

Democratic Republic of the
Congo

The Lingala word for sand is zε'lɔ

Before 1960, religious groups operated most of the schools in the Congo. Almost all of these schools were primary schools. The country had very few high schools or colleges. After independence, the Congolese government expanded its education system. It built high schools and colleges. Many years of violence have weakened the Congo's education system. The government has little money to fund education. Because of the cutbacks, school buildings have fallen apart. Teachers often go unpaid. Some have lost interest in their jobs and quit teaching. Students use out-of-date textbooks. Many parents cannot afford the required school fees.

Despite these troubles, about 45 percent of the people in the Congo have a primary education. About 30 percent have secondary schooling. About 21 percent of the population has had no schooling at all, and only about 3 percent of the population has attended college. The

❖ Not all Congolese children have the opportunity to attend school.

Over the years, violence has forced millions of Congolese people to move from their homes. Some leave their homes to avoid clashes or when armies approach their villages, but they return later. Some have moved permanently to find safety away from warring armies. Millions of children in the Congo have been affected by disease, malnutrition, and limited access to schools.

country's largest colleges are the University of Kinshasa and the University of Kisangani.

On average, Congolese students attend school for eight years. About two-thirds of Congolese older than 15 can read and write one of the nation's major languages. Many more males attend schools and colleges than females. More than 80 percent of males are literate, compared to only about 55 percent of females. Some Congolese believe that girls should stay home to help the family, though this attitude is changing.

CHAPTER FOUR

CELEBRATIONS!

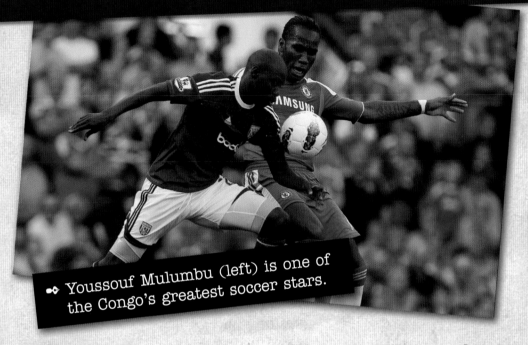

➻ Youssouf Mulumbu (left) is one of the Congo's greatest soccer stars.

What would you do for fun if you lived in the Congo? Although many Congolese have little time and money for celebrations, they enjoy playing or watching sports and celebrating holidays.

Like many people throughout the world, the Congolese love soccer, which they call football. Belgian colonists introduced the game to the Congo, and the country now has several professional leagues. Linafoot is the nation's top league. Mazembe, Motema Pembe, and Vita are its leading clubs. The Congo's national football team competes in international events. Nicknamed the Leopards, the national team won the Africa Cup of Nations competition in 1968 and 1974. The 1974 championship qualified the team for the 1974 World Cup. Although the team lost all three of its matches in the group stage, the entire nation celebrated the team's participation in the event. Congolese footballers play in top professional leagues around the world. Hérita Ilunga and Youssouf Mulumbu are two notable Congolese players who have played in other countries.

Belgian colonists also introduced volleyball and basketball to the Congo. Volleyball is a popular sport in schools, and interest in basketball has exploded. NBA All-Star Dikembe Mutombo is the best-known Congolese basketball player. The towering 7 foot 2-inch (218 cm) center was a renowned shot blocker and defensive player. He retired in 2009. Mutombo is also known for his charitable work in the Congo and other African countries. He contributed $15 million and raised millions more to build a modern hospital near Kinshasa. Opened in 2006, the Biamba Marie Mutombo Hospital is named in honor of Mutombo's mother.

Music is an important part of Congolese life. Friends often meet and listen to music. Two related styles of music are uniquely Congolese. Soukous is a style of music that features guitars, drums, thumb pianos, and traditional

Congolese instruments. It originated in the Congo in the 1940s. Its popularity soared in the 1960s, and today souk- ous remains popular in the Congo and throughout Africa. Kwasa kwasa is a faster version of soukous. It started as a dance song in Kinshasa in the 1980s.

Holidays are special days in the Congo. For many Congolese, they provide a rare chance to relax. Observing holy days and showing pride in their country offers the Congolese a break from the stresses of their everyday lives.

Because most Congolese are Christian, the traditional Christian holidays are important throughout the Congo. Good Friday, Easter, and Christmas are major occasions for

◆ Soukous is one of the Congo's most popular forms of music.

➟ Congolese people often enjoy celebrations and holidays in the company of friends and family members.

families to get together. Easter and Christmas often feature a special meal to celebrate the occasion. Christians in the Congo usually don't exchange gifts on Christmas.

Members of the Kimbanguist Church celebrate Christmas in May instead of December. They believe that Jesus Christ was born on May 25 rather than December 25. During their Christmas celebrations, Kimbanguists wear white and green. White symbolizes purity, and green represents hope. In larger cities, bands march through the streets playing songs. Worshippers follow the bands and come together at a meeting place to pray.

A big meal is served after the prayer service. People then sing songs and dance to music to celebrate the day.

Weddings are some of the biggest celebrations in the Congo. Congolese often celebrate marriages with parties that can last three to four days. They usually begin on Wednesday or Sunday afternoons.

In addition to religious celebrations, the Democratic Republic of the Congo has several national holidays. Commemoration of the Martyrs of Independence is observed on January 4. It honors the heroes who died for the country's independence. The anniversary of the nation's constitution is celebrated on June 24, and Independence Day is celebrated on June 30. Armed Forces Day (November 17) pays tribute to the nation's soldiers. Other official holidays include New Year's Day (January 1) and Labor Day (May 1).

Congolese Muslims celebrate Ramadan. During this monthlong observance, they do not eat or drink from sunrise to sunset. At the end of Ramadan, Muslims enjoy Eid al-Fitr. During this three-day event, people visit their families and enjoy a special meal, which usually includes meat.

Parents' Day is celebrated on August 1. This holiday allows families to honor their ancestors. Families visit the graves of dead relatives. They clean the headstones and gravesites of their loved ones. Then they enjoy a picnic lunch at the cemetery or another location. After lunch, they return home and spend the rest of the day enjoying quiet time together.

MAKE A KIFWEBE MASK

The Luba and Sonqye are two Congolese ethnic groups. They have used Kifwebe masks in various ceremonies and community events for centuries. Skilled woodworkers carve the masks from wood. You can make a simple Kifwebe mask using common craft materials.

MATERIALS

- One sheet of 8½ × 11 inch (21.6 × 28 cm) paper
- Pencil
- Scissors
- One piece of cardboard, about 12 × 12 inches (30.5 cm × 30.5 cm)
- Crayons, markers, or acrylic paint
- X-Acto knife
- 18 inches (46 cm) of string

INSTRUCTIONS

1. Use the Internet to find images of Luba and Sonqye Kifwebe masks. Choose one you like to use as a model.
2. On the sheet of paper, make a pencil drawing of how you want your mask to look. In addition to eyes, a nose, and sometimes eyebrows, Kifwebe masks feature patterns or shapes. Be sure to include these in your drawing.

3. Use scissors to cut off the unused edges of your drawing. You will use this drawing as a pattern for your mask.

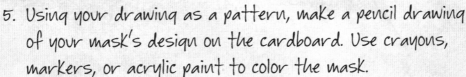

4. Place the cardboard against your face. Use the pencil to mark the location for the mask's eyes and mouth. Draw lightly to prevent the pencil from going through the cardboard.

5. Using your drawing as a pattern, make a pencil drawing of your mask's design on the cardboard. Use crayons, markers, or acrylic paint to color the mask.

6. With the assistance of an adult, use the X-Acto knife to cut out slits on the cardboard for your mouth and nose.

7. With the assistance of an adult, use the X-Acto knife to make a small hole on each side of the mask. Position the holes just above eye level and about $\frac{1}{2}$ inch (1.25 cm) from the edge.

8. Thread the end of the string through one hole and tie a knot at the end. Thread the other end of the string through the other hole. Place the mask on your face, with the string behind your head. Tighten the string so the mask won't fall off. Tie off the untied end of the string. Use the scissors to cut the excess string just above the knot.

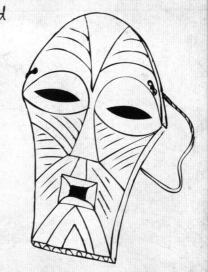

CHAPTER FIVE

WHAT'S FOR DINNER?

→ Yassa is one of the many delicious dishes served up by Congolese cooks.

Meals in the Congo are often based on dairy products and grains. Many Congolese foods contain a lot of **starch**. For breakfast, Congolese might drink milk or eat yogurt. They often do not eat anything else. They also eat a light meal in the evening. It usually consists of milk or yogurt or a starch served with broth or vegetables.

Lunch is usually the biggest meal of the day. It often consists of a stew known as a sauce. There are many different types of sauces. Some are made just with vegetables. Others include poultry, fish, or beans. Congolese cooks often add tomatoes, onions, and chili peppers to sauces. Stews made with ground peanuts are also popular. A peanut stew usually includes beef, chicken, or fish. It is served with cucumber, onion, and hard-boiled eggs.

Sauces are often served on top of a bed of corn or rice. The Congolese also eat starchy bread called *fufu* with their meals. Cooks use cassava, yams, millet, corn, or potatoes to make fufu. In homes, meals are served in a large bowl. The bowl is placed on a mat on the floor, and all of the diners eat from it. Men and women often eat separately.

The national dish of the Democratic Republic of the Congo is *moambé*. This is a spicy peanut sauce made with palm oil. Moambé is made with meat or chicken and served on rice. *Yassa* is another popular dish. Although originally from Senegal, it has been adopted by Congolese cooks. Yassa is chicken or fish that is marinated in lemon juice, grilled, and then fried with onions. Finally, it is simmered with the marinade until tender and served with rice.

Most Congolese consider meat a luxury. When they do eat meat, it is usually poultry—chickens, ducks, and guinea fowls. Fish are caught in lakes, rivers, or the Atlantic Ocean. Fresh fish are usually dried and salted

The cassava is a potato-like plant. Because it is easy to grow, cassava has become a staple food for millions of poor people in the Congo. It takes a lot of effort to prepare cassavas. First, their outer coating must be scraped off. Then the cassavas are soaked in water for several days. The soaked cassavas are cut into pieces and set out to dry in the sun. Finally, the brittle pieces of cassava are pounded into a powder. Cooks combine this powder with water to make fufu.

for eating later. In the rain forests and savannas, where meat is especially scarce, people hunt various wild animals. Popular meats are antelope, porcupine, wild pig, and monkey. They are known as bush meats.

You'll find many other foods in Congolese kitchens. Okra, beans, and a wide variety of greens are popular. Many cooks use palm oil when cooking meats and vegetables. This vegetable oil gives food a red color.

The Congolese drink many different beverages. In addition to sodas, they drink juices made from tamarinds, mangoes, or other fruits. *Karkadé* is a popular tea made with the dried flowers of the hibiscus plant.

Would you like to make a yummy Congolese dish? Moambé is the Congo's national dish. There are many different moambé recipes, but this one uses ingredients commonly found in North American grocery stores.

Chicken Moambé

INGREDIENTS
5 tablespoons (75 milliliters) palm oil
4 chicken breast halves, cut into
   medium chunks
1 medium onion, diced
1 tablespoon (15 ml) salt
½ teaspoon (2.5 ml) piri piri
   or other chili sauce
2 tablespoons (30 ml)
   peanut butter
4 cups (1 liter) water

INSTRUCTIONS

1. Pour 4 tablespoons of the palm oil into a deep pot. Add the chicken and onion. Use a spoon to mix the ingredients with the palm oil. Let the mixture sit for 5 minutes to allow the chicken and onion to absorb the oil.

2. Add the salt and piri piri sauce to the mixture and stir to combine the ingredients.

3. Cook the mixture on medium heat, turning the chicken pieces occasionally so that they cook on all sides.

4. Put the peanut butter and the remaining 1 tablespoon of palm oil into a medium bowl. Use a spoon to mash the ingredients together until you have a paste.

5. When the chicken pieces have browned, add the paste. Use a wooden spoon to mix thoroughly.

6. Add the water to the pot. Stir with the wooden spoon to mix the ingredients.

7. Bring the stew to a boil. Turn the heat to low. Let the stew simmer for at least 30 minutes.

8. Taste the dish and adjust the spices as desired.

9. Serve with cooked rice.

➜ Banana fritters are a tasty treat for the people of the Congo.

Desserts are not a traditional part of Congolese meals. Coconuts, papayas, mangoes, and other tropical fruits are popular treats, though. Fritters are another favorite snack. To make fritters, cooks coat bananas or pineapple chunks with flour and fry the mixture.

Whether you are enjoying a bowl of moambé or listening to the latest soukous tune, you will be fascinated and challenged by the Democratic Republic of the Congo. Influenced by its ancient history and struggling to overcome its current troubles, the Congo is a land of contrasts. It is both dense rain forest and wide-open savanna. It is bustling cities and remote wildernesses. Which parts of the Congo do you want to explore?

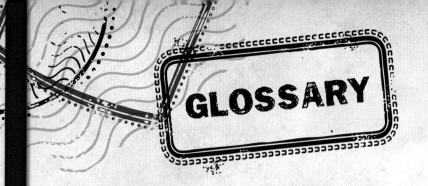

GLOSSARY

basin (BAY-sun) a bowl-shaped land formation

bribes (BRYBZ) money given to people to convince them to do something

cabinet (CAB-uh-net) a group of people who advise a country's leader

colony (KAH-luh-nee) a territory ruled by a foreign government

corruption (kuh-RUP-shuhn) a lack of integrity or ethical conduct

coup (KOO) a sudden, often violent, change in government leadership not achieved through an election or other standard political process

equator (e-KWAY-tur) an imaginary line around the earth, located halfway between the North Pole and the South Pole

ethnic (ETH-nik) having to do with a group of people sharing the same national origins, language, or culture

militias (muh-LISH-uhz) groups of soldiers who are not part of a nation's armed forces

primates (PRI-mayts) related mammals such as humans, monkeys, and apes

species (SPEE-sheez) one of the groups into which animals and plants are divided, based on their characteristics

starch (STARTCH) a tasteless, odorless, white substance found in foods such as potatoes, rice, and wheat

tributaries (TRIB-yoo-tare-eez) rivers or streams that flow into larger rivers

FOR MORE INFORMATION

Books

Barter, James. *The Congo*. San Diego: Lucent Books, 2003.

DiPiazza, Francesca. *Democratic Republic of Congo in Pictures*. Minneapolis: Twenty-First Century Books, 2008.

Heale, Jay, and Yong Jui Lin. *Democratic Republic of the Congo*. New York: Marshall Cavendish Benchmark, 2010.

Web Sites

Central Intelligence Agency: The World Factbook—Democratic Republic of the Congo
https://www.cia.gov/library/publications/the-world-factbook/geos/cg.html
Get up-to-date information about the Congo's government, people, geography, and economy.

National Geographic Music—Congo (DRC)
http://worldmusic.nationalgeographic.com/view/page.basic/country/content.country/congo_drc_zaire_17
Check out information on the Congo's vibrant music history.

USAID—Democratic Republic of Congo
www.usaid.gov/locations/sub-saharan_africa/countries/drcongo
Find information about current conditions in the Congo.

INDEX

animals, 12–13, 42

Bangweulu Swamps, 13
basketball, 34
Belgian Congo, 17, 18
borders, 6, 9

capital city, 6, 10, 27, 30, 32, 34, 35
cassava, 15, 25, 41, 42
children, 16, 32
cities, 6, 10, 17, 27, 30, 32, 34, 35
climate, 9, 11–12
Congo Free State, 16
Congo River, 6–7, 10, 11, 13, 14, 16, 20, 27
constitution, 22, 37
corruption, 22, 24
currency, 24

economy, 23–24, 26, 29, 30
education, 16, 30–32
elections, 18, 22
ethnic groups, 18, 20, 29, 38
executive branch of government, 18, 19, 21, 22
exploration, 11, 15, 16
exports, 26

families, 32, 36, 37
farming, 13, 15, 24–25, 29, 42
flag, 23
foods, 40–42, 43–44, 45

government, 16, 17, 18, 19, 21–22, 29, 30

health care, 16, 34
holidays, 35–37
housing, 32, 41

imports, 26
independence, 18, 30, 37

jobs, 17, 24, 31
judicial branch of government, 22

Kabila, Joseph, 21, 22
Kabila, Laurent, 21
Kasavubu, Joseph, 18
Kinshasa, 6, 10, 27, 30, 32, 34, 35
Kisangani, 27, 32
Kongo Kingdom, 14, 15
Kongo people, 11, 29

Lake Tanganyika, 6, 9, 10
land area, 5
languages, 29, 30, 32
legislative branch of government, 22
literacy rate, 32
Luba Kingdom, 14–15, 15–16
Lubumbashi, 27
Lumumba, Patrice, 18, 19
Lunda Kingdom, 14–15

maps, 7, 10
military, 16, 19, 20, 21, 23, 37
mining, 25, 26
missionaries, 16, 17
moambé (national dish), 41, 43–44
Mobutu, Joseph, 19, 20, 21
mountains, 6, 8–9, 10, 11, 27
Mulumbu, Youssouf, 34
music, 34–35, 36, 37

Muslims, 28–29, 37
Mutombo, Dikembe, 34

natural resources, 16, 23, 25
ngangas (spiritual healers), 29

plantations, 16
plants, 8, 12, 13, 16, 26, 29
population, 5, 6, 27, 28, 29
Portuguese explorers, 15
primates, 13

rain forests, 8, 13, 16, 42
refugees, 20
religion, 28–29, 30, 35–36, 37
rural areas, 17, 27
Rwenzori Mountains, 8

savannas, 8, 13, 42
slavery, 15–16, 17
sports, 33–34

timber industry, 26
transportation, 16, 25
trees, 8, 13, 26

Virunga Mountains, 8–9
volcanoes, 9

wetlands, 8, 13

ABOUT THE AUTHOR
G. S. Prentzas has written more than two dozen books for young readers. He has explored every continent except Antarctica. He hopes to visit the Democratic Republic of the Congo someday.